I LOVE YOU MOM,

BUT YOU AND I

ARE GETTING

A

DIVORCE

BY

DR. GAILE M. DALEY

FOREWORD

This book is about my experiences and the many things I've learned from living them. By sharing these things with you, my reader, I'm taking you through my journey to the release of the biggest toxic relationship in my life; my mother.

By reviewing the processes I went through and the steps that I took, I'll share with you the true self-esteem that I developed, nurtured, and maintained that allowed me to terminate the relationship with my mother.

My hope is that other people, who recognize either these or similar traits, can come to the place of releasing the most horrifying, toxic relationship from their life. They are horrifying because the relationship is with a direct family member.

An important intention is that the reader understand that releasing a toxic family relationship is not to be done out of anger, resentment, hatred, fear, disgust or any other negative emotion. The honoring of self and honoring that divine part of you should be the only reason we allow ourselves to release this toxic person from our lives. Otherwise, the toxic relationship is not necessarily clear and healed appropriately.

"Is it a New England thing?"

"It stinkin' looks that way based on others I have talked to."

This is a conversation I have had on a few occasions while talking to other girls about our experiences with our mothers.

We would laugh but I could sense the strain and grief from all of us in attendance.

I can remember a number of times getting together with other people, usually women, usually over alcohol, wherein we would engage in mom bashing.

We would go on about how we were raised and the things that our mothers said and did and demanded of us, and how much we all resented it. Frequently, everybody at the table would say, sometimes at the same time, "There must be a mom handbook somewhere out there. That's exactly how it goes in my house too!"

In my case, even though I had been this badass in the military and law-enforcement fields, my mother still had the ability to reduce me to a child, creating more anger and resentment within me even as an adult.

As humans we feel that we're supposed to place a lot of weight and value on family. Our sense is that we are not to betray them, and we are supposed to endure things because a person is in the role of a parent. Anyone who has gone through something similar to this can share numerous stories of their other siblings who try to persuade them to be nice to mom or dad or whoever in the family is not treating you well, because they are family.

So often, out of guilt, we stay someplace that's very disturbing to our inner strength and inner self, and ultimately our inner peace, because they are family.

I realized later in life that my mom exhibited the epitome of some toxic behaviors, such as criticism, judgment, control, manipulation, bullying, and acting like a victim to get her way. But the coup de gras was *the look*. This was the *boring into your soul* look that she projected at me while gritting her teeth and clenching her jaw.

It meant *you are displeasing mommy and you'd better start acting right.*

My response to this? *Anger*.

INTRODUCTION

I am from Upstate New York. Back in my day, that would often be a farm or a blue-collar town. My parents were from the same region near the capital district. They knew each other during their high school years. My mom was 22 years old when she gave birth to me and my dad was 21. Essentially, still kids themselves.

Both of my parents had been living with their respective parents and working at a job. My mom as a waitress, my dad as a farmhand first and then as a flooring installer.

Two years before I was born, they had my sister. Two years after me, another sister. I was 3 years old when my parents divorced. A few years later mom had a new husband and I had a brother. By the time I was10 years old my mother was raising four kids on her own and continued to do so throughout the 60's, 70's and early 80's.

My mother worked the split shift as a waitress nearly six days a week so I never saw her in the morning because she was still sleeping. My older sister (13 yrs old) and I (11 yrs old) got ourselves out of bed, fed, and off to school. We woke up the younger two kids (9 & 5 years old) who got themselves to the bus before mom woke up. I rarely saw mom before we went to bed because she worked until 8pm or later and her commute was a 20-minute drive home. I would see her on her day off and she was always fretting, most often silently.

My family did a lot of relocating while us kids were growing up to remove us from areas where we were making potentially bad decisions based on what other kids did and, truth be told, running from some creditors. I think I moved 9 times before I turned 18. My siblings and I had come to accept that we were pretty close to being *trailer trash*. Being left to raise ourselves, we were almost like wild animals. Thankfully, my mom was proud *and* narcissistic so I never completely got the T-shirt or belt buckle for being complete trash. Something deep inside of me was aware that my upbringing was not comfortable or usual. The amount of issues and events that my siblings and I sucked up to be able to tough out our existence is worthy of an award.

The incidences that I recall always involved all four of us kids being fearful. We lived in a sub remote location that we referred to as living out in the country. Our ages were 12, 10 (me), 8 and 4. My older sister had the brains and I had the brawn.

Once, while mom was at work 20 minutes away, my younger sister hit her head on the corner of a cabinet. She was bleeding pretty steadily so we knew enough to call mom at work. Mom was not allowed to have any phone calls go to her boss's office. We had to call her on the public pay phone (boy, did I just date myself), and we only called during emergencies. Anyone passing the phone booth could answer the phone. Most of the time mom was not told there was a call for her. Or maybe, in the fray of doing her waitress job, she simply forgot to go to the phone. My sister was bleeding from her head and all of us kids were near hysterical because we cannot reach her, so my older sister ran to the neighbor that lived two houses (~2 acres) away. We took my little sister to the neighbor and the neighbor applied the required first aid. Then we went home to clean up the mess and have the house neat for when mom came home. We informed mom of the entire incident. Mom became upset and checked on the younger sister and saw she was essentially fine. The stress, anxiety, and fear of all of us kids was never mentioned or addressed.

Another incident was over the top of anything that kids should have to handle. I was deemed the strong, silent one of the family because I had become more of an observer of people and life, not trusting that anybody had my back. I felt that the adults in my family were ridiculous. I had taken on the job of being the protector of everyone's physical and emotional states. One evening in the winter, my older sister and I heard a noise in the basement. The younger siblings were asleep and unaware. As usual, mom was working her waitress job, 20 minutes away from the house.

The reason why my sister and I were so worked up and concerned about a noise was because where we lived was just in front of the railroad tracks, out in the country. The older kids in the neighborhood had always regaled us with stories of hobos and other transients jumping off of the trains and going into people's yards. I had never in my four years of living there seen or heard directly about anyone having had that experience, but we were kids and naturally thought the stories were true.

Being the strong, silent one, I had to buck up and physically walk through the house to investigate. Now remember, I'm in grammar school and while I didn't want to, I did it for all of our survival. Turns out I found nothing, but the fear remained through the night. I don't remember if I slept and nothing was said to mom because by the time we saw her it was in the past and nothing had happened. We weren't hiding anything from her. It's just that we thought these things were normal. Who knew?

Because of all the stressors my siblings and I endured and the absence of my mom, when she had her day off, I did not want her around. I definitely didn't want her to tell me what to do or how I should do something. I got shit figured out. My siblings and I were surviving and doing well.

I particularly resented mom when she would criticize me. "Why don't you pull your hair away from your face? Why don't you work at raising the octave of your voice? Why don't you take a foreign language in school, like your sister? Why is your singing voice so low? Why don't you get your ears pierced? Why don't you dress more feminine?" She would also ask, "Why don't you have your friends over?" and I thought "I don't want anyone to see this circus!" This was the beginning of my retreating from being wounded by her. It was breaking my self-esteem.

While mom was doing this to me it had me feeling pretty low. Now, some people may have retreated and become shy, maybe even depressed. My reaction was to go to anger. I used that anger to prove to myself, and others, that I was capable and worthy.

Mom was pretty vain in her outer appearance. When we were around others she would demonstrate a very charming and flirtatious side and it made me cringe knowing it was a show. She had two distinct sides to her and she was particularly *on* when she was around men. It made me angry because I saw the falseness.

If you asked me, my mom's emotional development stopped at about 9-14 years old. She pretty much lived in a fantasy world. She was a brilliant woman and if guided by driven and successful people could have been a brain surgeon. Instead, based on her generation and influences, all she really wanted was to marry a successful man that could provide financially and emotionally for her and her kids. She would have preferred to be exceptionally well dressed, with her exceptionally well mannered and well dressed children, walking hand in hand through downtown to eat lunch at Woolworths. Oops! Did I just date myself again?

I found this woman to be a mess and I was frustrated with it all. From the time I was about 13 years old, I could not wait to turn 18 so I could move out of her house.

Where was Dad in all of this? We had visitation with dad every other Sunday. Once in a while my sister or I would speak about some activities at the house that we were frustrated with or thought were ridiculous. What we didn't realize was that he was discussing these things with his new wife. A day came where my dad asked us girls if we wanted to live with him. We said, "Mom wouldn't allow that." When he approached my mom, in front of us girls no less, my mom said "No." I was secretly relieved because I knew that at my dad's house, I would not have gotten away with the shenanigans I pulled while mom wasn't watching.

We moved out of the country and back into the city when I was 14 years old. From 14-18 years old, I was just trying to stay away from the house and mom. Mostly what I remember about mom was when she was home, at the end of her day or on a day off, reading the newspaper, looking at TV occasionally, sleeping, eating dinner with us, and in the evenings consuming liquid fermented grapes.

While biding my time, waiting to turn 18 years old, I respected my mom, but I can't say I really enjoyed being around her. To this day, I still have issues with anyone saying what sounds like my mom's demands to me, "You need to . . .You have to . . . You really should . . .Why don't you . . ."

The prospect of her saying any of those things kept me at a distance from her. I could not articulate it then, but I believe that I was feeling like I wasn't living up to her standards.

A little about me. As a young person, I did not have any point of reference to explain why I had a subtle feeling of shame and of being flawed. Thankfully, I had some childhood gifts and activities that served as coping mechanisms by separating me from my family environs.

I was, and still am, very connected to nature and animals. I realized at a young age that I am a telepathic empath and an animal communicator. Because of this, I spent as much time as possible being outdoors. I still do. Otherwise, I feel contracted and irritable inside.

Later in life, I would become a board-certified animal chiropractor. Talk about a non-job! It was a dream come true.

I got through high school okay enough. I worked for a year before going to a two-year college. I received an associate degree in criminal justice at the local community college and I started to feel like I was preparing myself to be worthy. I started focusing on opportunities to get out of town. We had grown up fast on some level, but I can't say we were emotionally mature. But we had endured!

OBSERVATIONS OF AN OUTSIDER

Four and a half decades later and still his words stick with me. Whose words? The medical doctor at the Veterans Administration Clinic in Syracuse, NY, who performed the initial exam on me after being honorably discharged from the U.S. Air Force.

Four years earlier, I had gone into the military to gain career experience and to escape home. I finished my military tour at 26 years of age and immediately applied for a disability rating for the injury I sustained while on active duty. During the application process, there was a physical exam by a VA doctor to determine my eligibility.

Having never been comfortable in hospitals or large offices, I was smiling and giggling out of nervousness when the doctor called me to the exam room. The doctor asked me many questions while conducting his exam on my left knee.

I watched the doctor write notes in my chart and saw him write *Gaile is a well-adjusted person* and I never forgot those words or my inner reaction: "Well adjusted? What else would I be? Doesn't everyone live a life similar to mine? What other options are there?"

Was I really well adjusted? No. Had I mastered the use of smoke and mirrors to get through life? Yes. I used/created smoke and mirrors as coping mechanisms and to stand up to my mother. I continued to use them for decades because they helped me keep other people at arm's length so that I would not be emotionally hurt by them too.

I used them to mask my hurt and grief and fears. Anger, shock value, comedy, intimidation, and working out to build muscle and strength is how I coped. Essentially, I acted tough and sarcastic. I said things to cause people to think and feel that it would not be a good idea to mess with me.

I added stoicism and standoffishness to keep people at arm's length. I was trying to avoid more emotional hurts by making a show of physical prowess and verbal intimidation. Truth be told, these were covering up hurts and fears that were pushed down very, very deep.

At some point I started to use comedy and loud, boisterous behaviors to get people to believe I was fun. I later sensed that I may have been doing it to get people to like me because I didn't know how to be comfortable being my true self yet. I had a deep feeling inside that people could see my shame and flaws. I spent years pretending to be unflappable and steady because I had not yet allowed myself to see that I had to accept the true me first.

Fast forward, 32 years.

THE NAME OF MOM'S GAME WAS SHAME

It finally occurred to me when I was 58 years old that the word for the dynamics and behaviors my mother had demonstrated to me and my siblings was **shame**.

I had just walked into my kitchen and heard my inner voice say *shame*. I asked my voice what this meant, and I clearly heard "That's the word you have been searching for that explains what your mother does to you."

I burst into tears. I did that ugly face crying that we do during a deep pain.

What does *shame* mean to me? It means breaking the spirit of an individual, human or animal. After that realization, I had a peace come over me because of the clarity I had just gained.

I was truly grateful for this new understanding. Knowing there was a word for it meant to me that other people were probably experiencing it.

Mom spent her entire life shaming each of her children.

As she got older, approaching her late 70s, she felt that it was acceptable because she had earned the right as an elderly person, to go ahead and shame others that she encountered.

All through my life I had always wondered why I could not stand to be in mom's company. I especially disliked talking to her on the phone. It was while we were on the phone that she would be even more brutal because she was essentially out of arms reach, assuming that my siblings and I would not demand to be treated as adults and with respect.

This is the person who had always said, "I am your mother and that's why you need to do what I tell you to do and act the way I tell you to act." I can't tell you how many times I told her over the years that just because she gave birth to me did not afford her any divine right to continue to treat me like a child and to disrespect me.

I look at the dynamics of the parent child relationship each time I speak to people and observe their relationships. Regardless of their age, I often find that shaming theme.

What do I mean by shaming? If you were frequently (if not constantly) criticized for the way you look, talk, the way you wear your hair, the friends you have, the job that you have, etc., then you were shamed. If you were shamed in childhood and into adulthood, people become so used to it that few recognize the dynamic. All they knew was that they felt bad around the shaming parent.

Constant criticism is shaming, and my mother constantly criticized me. When I would stand up and set a boundary and demand that she notice the way that she was interacting with me, her explanation always was, "Well, I am your mother, and I am just looking out for what is best for you."

I constantly felt reduced to a child because I never measured up to her expectation of how I should live my life. I came to realize many decades later that this was *her* shortcoming, not mine. Her problem, not mine. And while I'd hear "Your mother did the best she could with what she had" and I realized that was probably true, it did not excuse or remove the damage done.

My mother would say to me "I forbid you to get a motorcycle." Or, "Why do you have to be a cop? This displeases me." And when I was assigned as a federal agent in Michigan I heard, "When are you moving back home?" I would tell her that I was home wherever I lived. She would respond that it wasn't acceptable to her. My personal favorite was when she would pout and say "Why are you doing this to me? Don't you want to live near me?" That would totally inflame me. She was always looking for validation and attention.

Truly, I do know that she was interacting with me and others in this shaming manner because she was most likely shamed herself as a child, and quite possibly the generation before her experienced that same pattern. My mother's family is German and a little Irish with a long line of alcoholism and spousal abuse. Women didn't have a voice and men were always between jobs. The jobs they worked were all lower income and blue collar. Mom would say that her father's mother was a very nasty Irish woman and between this woman and her daughters she felt almost Cinderella-ish.

She shared a story with me once about when her parents were at a bar and she was told over the phone, "Make sure that Rusty stays indoors after school." Rusty was her brother and she was 14 and Rusty was 12. She would be derided when they finally returned from the bar and saw that Rusty was not in the house.

Another story she told me was that her alcoholic father would say sexually inappropriate things to her. He would read books to her and ask her "Are your panties wet?" She also relayed to me that when she was about 9 years old, while visiting her elementary school aged cousins, they would tell her she was worthless, unwanted, and ugly.

Time and time again I would speak to mom about a different way to approach me, a different way to observe and accept me. She would say that she likes things the way that she does them and that only her way is acceptable to her.

As a young person, I made numerous attempts to individuate myself by setting boundaries. Once was at about 8 years old when my family was in a department store and my mom stopped at a clothing rack. She turned to me and said, "Gaile, do you like this? I do." I responded with a "No" and she spun her head around and gave me such a look of anger. That look was meant to control me and change my mind to match her opinion.

I recall thinking that she was pissed, and she'd just have to deal with it. Still, inside me, I knew that once again I was not accepted by mom and her love and appreciation of me was again removed.

That was the first time that I stood up for myself against her attempts to control and manipulate. I was respectful to her even though I did not want to be.

That look of anger she gave me was meant to control me. My siblings and I always referred to that as when mom gives you *the look*.

She used it to clearly show you how displeased mommy was with you, and you'd better straighten up and go with what mom wants.

Truthfully, it only worked on one of my sisters. The rest of us kids just walked away, silently feeling unapproved of. Luckily, us kids had each other and the support we provided helped maintain us emotionally. It took me years to realize that my other emotion was the realization that her love was conditional. Years later I realized something deeper was happening in me. I was experiencing tremendous grief at her love being conditional and the shaming and control tactics she used. As a kid I had no articulations or point of reference to define what was going on in me. It was just something else I *sucked up*.

At 14 years old, I further individuated myself from my mom by lying to her about where I was going when I left the house. I said I would be at a friend's house but actually I would walk, by myself, all around town. Other times, I would also tell her stories of things that I would say to other people with a lot of shocking details that I would make up just to get her wondering if she really knew what I was capable of. Everyone else would laugh but I could see mom starting to wonder about me. Mission accomplished.

She would not honor my request to be treated differently while I was living in her house. Actually, she never honored my request to be respected and treated like an adult. I became a very angry and frustrated individual. When she acted like a victim I saw her as unfair and weak. A bully. She was not kind. I knew by my mid teens that I did not want to continue the cycle of her behaviors.

I WANT THE TRUTH AND NOTHING BUT THE TRUTH

I don't remember how old I was but I'm pretty sure I was in junior high school when I realized that my mother was the queen of embellishing. Later on I would describe this as realizing that I really could not believe anything that my mother was saying.

She would speak in a critical, judgmental, and bullying manner regarding other people and she managed to make these people and situations out to be absolutely deplorable. One such lambasting was regarding my father.

Mom said, "Your father was immature and weak. He would cry to me when he didn't have a job or the bills were coming due. I was always the strong one, telling him it was ok. I'm the one who got him a great job, taught him how to dress better, and how to stand up for himself. Do you know that his family doesn't even have a bathroom inside the home?"

Even at my young age I was thinking, "What nerve!" I realized that another reason she did this was because she would be holding court with her children – our attention and eyes were on her. She was the focus. And she was always smiling while she said these things. She loved to be the focus of everyone's attention.

The upshot of anything that my mother said was essentially that other people were less than her and that other people were always wrong no matter what they did, said, wore, where they worked, or what they drove.

My mother was always telling endless stories of how she was the victim in life and that others never showed her appreciation, if not clearly came out and told her that she was deplorable herself or that she was disgusting.

I was always struck by the fact that my mother never cried while talking about these things. Myself, I would have found it heartbreaking.

To this day my mother still says, "I have never been loved." Any one of us kids present would immediately exclaim, "Are you kidding me? I am standing right here! We always express our love both verbally and through actions. You have the audacity to make this claim? You know that you are just trying to get others to feel bad for you!"

Mom's coworkers would see any number of us kids at social events and tell us what my mother had been saying about her childhood and her life. The coworker would say that most of the people at the workplace felt bad for my mother and were giving her hugs and a shoulder to cry on and they were pretty sure that mom had a tough life. When these things were said in front of me, I would tell the coworker, "You can bet that it is a huge manipulation to get attention!"

I DIDN'T HAVE CHILDREN BECAUSE

All through my childhood and teens, I did not have a relationship with my mother that I would describe as nurturing or a real relationship. Her characteristics of acting like a victim and shaming and bullying caused me to see her as being very false. I can't tell you the number of times that I wished I would not run into her during the course of a day.

To be clear, I am not telling you that every moment with my mother was some kind of a crap show. It was not. But when she would speak to me in her demanding, self-righteous, narcissistic, and childlike way I could not stand being around her.

In my early 20s I went into the military. It was the first time I had ventured out on my own. I was stationed at a location that was not within my mother's daily reach. My mother carried on like this was going to end her life and she asked me "Why are you doing this to me?" Of course, it had nothing to do with her and it frustrated me further that she could not be happy with my moving forward with a purpose.

Now I have always been aware that there is a bit of a sociologist within me. I have always been the type of person that enjoyed observing people in their words and actions and how they got through their day. As early as middle school years I was able to take note of people and their behaviors and feel that something was normal or abnormal, good or not good. By high school, I had a big sense of this personality cycle that I saw in my mother and her parents and even previous generations. I felt strongly that this cycle should end, and I knew for a fact that it would not be continued through me.

Being as angry and frustrated as I was as a child, teenager, and in my 20s and 30s, I knew that my dynamics and personality characteristics would be a very magnified presentation of what I had been living every day. I felt that I would break my child's spirit every day and that I would potentially be even worse at shaming and bullying my children than even my mother had been. I was angrier than anyone else in my family appeared to be. So, every time I would be asked if I had children, and then why I didn't have children, I always replied with "I didn't have children because I knew that I was too selfish and impatient to have children."

People who knew my personality thought this additional explanation was funny. It was, I thought, a very picturesque, flashy explanation. I would tell people that since I'd been in the military and a cop, I envisioned myself as the parent with children standing at attention, as I bark orders at them, wearing highly polished military jump boots, with the tips of those very polished boots flush with the painted line on the floor that I demanded that they line up on.

As I was going for *shock value* with that description, it always scored.

At the age of 31 I had a surgical procedure to ensure I would never had children. When I told my older sister what I was going to do she sounded panicked. She thought I would regret it one day. She was just interjecting her own feelings. I have never regretted my decision.

Over the years I have calmed down and come to a place of less anger in my life, so even though I enjoy other people's children for short periods of time, I still do not lament my

decision to not have them.

I BECAME A BADASS COP

Before I became a board-certified animal chiropractor I had a whole other life. I spent my early 20s in the military. I used the military route to gain job experience because for years I knew that I wanted to become a police officer. I also used it to get away from home.

Even though I had hit the age of 21 and had a little bit of college under my belt, the police departments were still requiring some previous experience. For me, that meant going into the military. I chose the Air Force because I did not feel I was man enough to be a Marine and the Navy said that I would need to do two years out at sea before being considered for my chosen field of law enforcement. At my young and naive age, I just assumed that people in the Army were the ones that were sent to war. The Air Force was going to give me a guaranteed contract to go into law enforcement out of basic training, so that's the choice I made. Additionally, I was looking for discipline and something that was going to give me respect and provide structure, and the military fit the bill.

From a very young age I developed a sarcastic and standoffish personality as a coping mechanism for the anger and frustration I felt during my early years. I also came across as tough and unflappable. So when I went into the military, that anger and frustration I carried with me had a way of making me appear confident. I was the strong silent type and it fit the military role very well.

I found it easy to do this because I was not surrounded by my birth family. It was not a situation where I was dependent on a loving heart connection. It was only a job.

My career in the Air Force was as a Law Enforcement Specialist and Sniper Team Leader for the Emergency Services Team on base. This was perfect for me because now I could act like a badass with all the authority that came with the badge and the gun and the titles. Within that law enforcement mode, I was enforcing the rules of the military and the laws of the U.S. I was highly decorated and received many commendations.

Admittedly, there were times during my military assignment where I used a little more physical persuasion or verbal intensity than was necessary. I figured that because I had the badge, the gun, the title, and that strong inner fortitude that I displayed with anger and smart mouth, I could get away with it. I never physically hurt anybody, but I will admit there were times that I behaved like a prick and a jerk.

Years later I experienced considerable guilt over my actions because there was truly no good excuse for doing what I did. It was as if I was showing off to other people so that I would get what I thought was respect. I know now that it was probably embarrassment and pity.

After my time in the military I went into federal law enforcement as a U.S. Marshal. With the military and law enforcement time under my belt, and still feeling angry and frustrated, I was thinking I was a pretty big deal. I continued with my badass attitude. And since I had created and maintained a very muscular and lean physique during my law enforcement years, I was the complete, formidable package.

By this time, I was in my early 30s. I had been living on my own since I was 21 and my mother was still making demands on me and my time that may have been fulfilling for her, but not for me. The demands were that I call her every Sunday.

Each week I would be ragingly angry with my mother and I would be resentful as hell and very much not looking forward to talking to her on the weekend. But still I did not have a handle on why I felt like I did, nor did I have the words to express how I felt. After a particularly intense performance by my mother, I realized just how much I resented this woman.

The performance by my mother occurred when my older sister and I decided to talk to mom about how she treated us. My sister Karen is two years older than me and lived in the same town as mom so the three of us communicated frequently. Karen and I would complain to each other weekly about mom's personality and antics. We were both absolutely embarrassed and frustrated at the victim position and manipulations that mom projected. Karen and I decided that we would have a calm, mature, and structured conversation with mom about the things she did and said and how it made others (mainly us) feel.

We asked mom to sit with us in the living room so we could talk to her. Mom was interested in the gathering in the living room because she thought she was going to be asked for advice or be told some juicy piece of information that she ultimately would take an inappropriate interest in, even though it was not going to be any of her business. What happened next was epic and looking back I realize that we should not have been surprised.

Karen and I felt that we had chosen our words and intentions very carefully because *God forbid we upset mom*!

Karen opens with, "Mom? Gaile and I want to have a calm, mature conversation with you about your actions and how you treat us." And *HOLY SHIT*! She stands up abruptly and shrieks while running to the kitchen in the back of the house, "What? You're blaming me for your feelings? You have no idea what I do for you kids. It's not easy for me. Do you know how hard it is for a woman my age to get a new job?" Now she was a very successful, long-term waitress at a very successful 5-star restaurant. Neither my sister nor I mentioned anything about a job, or money. We were going to focus on her interactive behaviors. Her reaction was an antic to distract us from the crux of the conversation's purpose. It was quite a performance!

Karen followed our mother into the kitchen to continue the conversation and pleaded with our mom to settle down and listen. I yelled to Karen to leave her alone and see the performance for what it was.

Karen walked back into the living room and mom is following behind her in hysterics and yells, "You have no idea what I go through. I work so hard to provide for you!" She is yelling this as she launches herself down the stairs and out onto the sidewalk. She has made herself absolutely inconsolable so she can be viewed as a huge victim.

In less than 5 minutes, with dry eyes and calm composure, she returns to the living room and says, "I don't want to talk about this anymore." I realized that this chick ain't right and I was impressed with her ability to burn through tears and hysterics with such speed and skill. I don't think we knew what to do after such an outburst and it was never mentioned again. I don't know what thought was in Karen's head, but I was wondering if there was anyone ever more fake than my

mother.

THAT IS WHAT FAMILY IS FOR

As I was growing up with my siblings, I recall them all saying that when they got married and had children that they were never, ever going to repeat the attitudes and dynamics of the family. Especially the shaming that my mother did.

When my sister Karen finally had children, she tried the other extreme and provided what I'm sure she felt was the opposite of what we grew up with. I'm sure it was a struggle for her. Karen gave her children a lot of freedom and room to grow and be who they were meant to be. They could express their emotions without reprisal. They got to choose their clothes, etc. One day while at Karen's house I saw her 3-year-old daughter walking across the top of the jungle gym in their backyard. If that were to occur today parents would be dialing 911 but Karen was perfectly relaxed with the situation. I was too since Karen was a nurse and her husband a PA, they at least knew where the hospitals were. To this day, Karen still has appropriate boundaries and an open relationship with her kids that I think a lot of parents would be envious of.

The damage done to all of us by our family dynamics and the coping skills we had all created, were very evident to me. Of the four of us, I was the only one not to have children. Watching siblings raise my nieces and nephews exposed me to an intriguing yet very personal sociology experience and had I not gone into law enforcement I would have become a sociologist. I was simply fascinated with it.

In my 20s, my awareness was growing daily, and I was experiencing clarity about what I was feeling, and why I was feeling it. I began to think about what I could be doing to change it. I noticed more and more how my siblings were affected and what they were doing with their interpretations. As I progressed through my anger, frustration, and how I used smoke and mirrors to deal with my guilt, shame, anger and hurt, I was noticing the effect on my siblings. And the more progress I made, the more I noticed how others, outside of my family unit, were dealing with their own family relationships.

One case stands out. My niece had incurred a physical assault at the hands of her stepfather and when she told her brother about it, he refused to believe her and sided with the stepfather because it was simply too upsetting for her brother to deal with the information.

When this niece would go to family functions, she would be fearful and angry knowing that she was going to run into her sibling who did not believe her. When I would ask her why she continued to have a relationship with her brother, her explanation was one word: *family*.

I said to my niece, "Just because this brother is your family member does not mean that you need to have a relationship with him. If another person who was not family had those same personality characteristics and also betrayed you like your brother, would you allow them to be a friend or an acquaintance in your life?" Her answer was a resounding **NO**!

As I progressed through all the work I did to clear myself of mom's shaming tactics I got stronger and stronger. And each time someone shared a story about a family member betraying them and the pain of having them still in their life, I'd ask that same question; "If it wasn't family, would you allow that person to be in your life?"

In the May 2019 issue of *O Magazine*, Oprah Winfrey made some statements regarding the death of her mother and how she was having a very difficult time forgiving her mom for how she was raised. Even though she had forgiven other people throughout her lifetime.

I have always thought that anybody who makes it onto the *Oprah Winfrey Show* is made in their business or product.

Here is a dynamic, real, direct, successful, courageous person, whom I have always found to be very inspiring, who is coming forward to talk about her mother, and her apparent inability to get totally free and clear from her interpretation of how her mom raised her. I imagine it might still be causing difficulty in Oprah's life. It was incredibly powerful to hear Oprah talk about it openly.

THE STRONGHOLD MOM HAD ON US

It was in my early 30s when the time had finally come for me to address my responses to my mom's shaming, manipulation, and control, as well as her victim and bully personality characteristics.

Regularly I would lay down to go to sleep and my head would be absolutely flooded with situations I had gotten involved in during the day that had brought me to a place of anger or frustration or even fear. I would then move to thoughts and memories about how resentful I was of my mother. Her shaming me, her manipulations, and her attempts to control me and how she acted like a victim when she pretended to cry, all of this caused a boat ton of distress within me.

I experienced tremendous feelings of guilt, responsibility, and obligation to be the good child and not upset the apple cart. A lot of those feelings were imposed upon me by my siblings attacking me because I was making mommy upset. I was not playing nice or fair, and I was causing upset and distress by standing forward and fighting for my own inner peace. After all, *why can't I just let mom be happy*?

I realized that in my family, and quite possibly other families, there is an absolute lack of boundaries within the house. When I attempted to create boundaries, I was seen as a traitor to the family, and that was not going to be allowed. After all, I opened the hall closet, wheeled out the family skeletons, put them in a chair on the porch, and gave them a glass of bourbon and a cigarette for all to see.

What an incredible stronghold this manipulative, narcissistic, angry person had. She had made it so that her children emotionally attacked each other if mommy was not happy. Mom also had us kids telling the gossip of the other siblings because mom *l-o-v-e-d* drama. Then mom would lord your baggage over your head when she spoke to you next. You know that is absolutely messed up!

Meanwhile I was losing more and more sense of who I was put here on the planet to be. Many is the time that any combination of myself or a sibling or two of mine would get together and we would all get to complaining about mom.

Mom did this and *mom said that,* and we would all express our anger and disgust and resentment and yet the next week, even though unwillingly, each of us would go ahead and call her. If you thought for a minute you were going to "show her" and not call her for a week, you can be sure that no matter which one of us siblings made that decision the call was made to mom the following week.

CHOOSING TO GET OFF THE WHEEL

Am I blaming my mom on everything that is wrong in my life? No. We all know that my mother's parenting skills had been shaped by how she was parented. But my problem came from how she continued to manipulate and control and shame me as I became an adult. From the time that I was out of the house at 21 years old she never treated me as an adult. She would always lord her power and manipulative mastery over me. She was a very strong personality. She had a tremendous stronghold on me from all the guilt and shame over feeling bad for mommy.

I had a huge problem with how she would continue to control and manipulate by making exclamations of being depressed, or how she couldn't go on, or how she had no reason to live, if any one of us no longer showed an interest in maintaining contact with her. God forbid you let two weeks go by without *reporting in*.

When it got close to the time I would have to call her, I was full of resentment and anger. The only reason I would continue to talk to her, or let her talk to me, was out of guilt and the feeling of responsibility and obligation that she had instilled in me as a child.

My siblings and I were not the only targets of mom's shaming and criticism. I remember numerous times while out shopping or at a restaurant when mom would be so embarrassing I would want to leave her wherever we were.

For instance, we would be at a restaurant and she would say to the waitress, "I don't like where the bench is by the door. You need to move it." Or, "The color of your uniforms is not becoming. You need to change that." Or, "You know I come in on Thursdays and Beverly is the only waitress that I like. You need to make sure she is here and not on a day off."

You could see the shock on the waitress' face and the embarrassment on mine.

Finally, though it took years to get there, I allowed myself to realize that this woman was toxic. The relationship and dynamics were just *so* not right. The manipulations of this woman were award winning. This is why I decided that there would be no more of this in my life.

When I finally allowed myself to move forward into honoring my inner peace as a divine being, I asked myself this question: "Would I allow someone who was not a family member, who possessed this same kind of dynamics and characteristics, whether a friend or an acquaintance or a coworker, to be part of my life?"

The answer was a resounding **NO**.

Immediately, I began a shoulder shuttering cry and the beginnings of starting to feel free.

MY STORY

In my early 30s I was living in Michigan where I was assigned as a U.S. Marshal. I had kidded myself into thinking that because I lived far away from mom she would ease up on me. Not a friggin' chance!

I would lie down to sleep at the end of a physically and probably emotional day, thinking I would fall fast asleep. Guess what actually happened? I'd lie there wide-awake thinking of all my mom's related drama and trauma because of that stronghold of guilt and shame she had instilled in her children. I would go over previous scenarios and rework them in my head, to my advantage. I would already be regretting the upcoming weekend call.

Do you know that if I didn't call at the time and date she thought that I should, she would yell at me? She would use that tone of voice and I just knew that she was clenching her jaw and giving me that glaring stare that was supposed to make me do her bidding and kowtow to her demands. I hated her for those actions.

One Monday morning after months of restless nights I made a call to my medical doctor to see who my health insurance plan would cover for some mental health counseling. I recall the doctor's nurse asking me "Are you thinking of hurting yourself?" I thought, "No, it's not me that is going to get hurt." When the therapist's office called me to make an appointment, they asked me the same question. I gave the same answer and laughed. I can imagine the look on the receptionist's face of "That girl needs an appointment with us yesterday!!" I suppose keeping my sense of humor has kept me protected and calm over the years.

Initially I started out with the traditional western medical model of going to see a social worker therapist. This enabled me to start to see a map of the coping mechanisms that I had created to get through my day. I had used anger, frustration, sarcasm, smart mouth, and just generally being formidable as a way to get through my day. Counseling helped me to understand that the anger was actually masked fear.

What were these masked fears? The fears were formed as a child in response to the feelings that I was on my own because I believed I wasn't living up to normal standards. That I felt rejected and was not being respected. I felt as though I was not good enough to be loved or taken care of.

As a very young person I always had an inner knowing that I had been put on the planet with some sort of skills or knowledge that would come to light as I got older. I just didn't know what the words or things were, but I did have a sense that I just needed to stay on my current course in life and things would expose themselves when it was time. I also realized at that very young age that I had many gifts. I am an animal communicator, a tremendous empath, and an intuitive healer for both people and animals.

It was in my early 30s when I realized I both needed and wanted to address my responses to years of shaming, manipulation, control and the personality characteristics of my mother acting like a victim and a bully.

I was about 18 years old when it became quite clear to me that I would make many changes over my lifetime in order to get to where I would free myself of *old ways* so I could be what my higher power, God, had put me on the planet to be. I had no idea what those events and changes would be. I can say now that I never felt like I was leading a *small* life. One thing necessary for me to move forward was to get my mom out of my life. I was 38 years old and still a U.S. Marshal in Michigan when I was furious enough at my mom to remove her from my life. I kept her out of my life for over thirteen years. She tried to go through my siblings to get info about me, hoping to tug at my heart.

Truth be told, I removed mom from my life due to my anger and dislike for her. Truly the wrong reason since it was not an emotionally healthy completion, and so I still felt guilt and obligation. I fought those emotions daily.

I had to get myself emotionally healthy. I used counseling and other methods to uncover my truths and realize that I was not flawed and had nothing to be ashamed of.

Thirteen years later, I had let mom back into my life and gone to her house for a visit even though she'd already started going back to her old ways of behaving. I admit, I was in denial. Between the trauma of being in her presence, being back home, and coupled with her cigarette smoke, I could not take it and went to a motel. My mom was put off that I was leaving her house and tried to talk me out of it. For the first time ever, I set a boundary and mom hated it.

My flight home was the next day and my older sister called me when I got home. She started yelling at me and said that mom had called her, upset. My sister yelled at me "Why couldn't you have just stayed at her apartment? After all, mom made a special meal for you and you couldn't be bothered to stay and eat it? And that's not all, mom went out of her way cleaning and bought new curtains for your visit because she was so excited! Couldn't you have just put up with her drama and the cigarette smoke?"

I told Karen to mind her own business, and that if she wanted to continue to do as mom wanted her to do, even though she hated it, to go ahead and do that. But I was not going to be uncomfortable and unhappy.

I was not in traditional mental health therapy for more than a year and a half before I began branching out to find other types of practitioners that could help me. During the early phases of looking for the right healing and clarity for me so I could clear up the deep levels of issues I had, I was talking to an intuitive guide about the feelings of fear and guilt I had regarding my mom.

I related to this intuitive guide something my mother had said when I was in junior high school which I had interpreted as my mom indicating that her life was so horrible she was considering suicide. I had never forgotten or let go of that fear that one day mommy would end up killing herself.

The practitioner said to me, "How old is your mother now?" I replied, "She is 68." The practitioner snapped her head around and looked at me and said, "So, you're saying that this woman who makes your life stressful, who controls and manipulates you and others, might commit suicide? How about you see that she is a master of control and she feeds on the distress of others? She won't commit suicide, she gets too much thrill from her power of manipulation!"

I almost fell over.

Ultimately, I found one of the things that worked very well for me was to pursue courses and books, seminars and practitioners, that could work with me on very deep levels, levels that could be coined as *spiritual* or *energy* work.

Through individual sessions with a practitioner, or a group setting at seminars, I developed many tools over the years to help me come to a place of acceptance and understanding of myself. The tools gained were through some of the courses I took which were Insight Seminars I through IV (InsightSeminars.org) and Soul Focused Transformational Healing.

I learned how to be a better person overall, how to be in a place that served me best and to be that person who is both loving and accepting with tremendous inner peace. It is my inner peace that is the most important factor to me in being of loving service. The changes I was making allowed me to change my inner responses to my mom's personality and behavior and so from 1993 to 2005 I managed to divorce my mother. This allowed me to no longer feel resentment and anger and the dislike that I felt towards her.

But, as much as I enjoyed not having mom in my life, and while I knew it was best for me to have complete removal of her from my life, I was still not strong enough and clear enough to not experience guilt and obligation. Imagine how disappointing that was to realize!! And do you know why that is? Because most of us humans, when we have a conflict with a loved one, very often go to a place of living in hope. Hope that the person will apologize, hope that the person will see the error of their ways. Hope that the person will realize how important we are in their life. Hope that the other person will change.

Hope is full of expectation!

And that can be so disappointing.

I realized that I still had a lot of work to do within me to be clear and to have total inner peace.

I would quickly bring myself back to center as I got faster at recognizing where I was out of balance and then use one of my tools to get myself back to balance.

And so, the work started again, more fervently this time.

More years went by and I continued with courses, gaining tools on how to recognize my characteristics and how I responded to life and its situations.

There was a huge epiphany when it was brought to my attention that what I really, truly, needed to do was to start being my true self on the planet.

Standing forward in the truth of who I am - a loving and compassionate child of a higher power and a healer doing fulfilling works and being of service on the planet - helped me tremendously to relax and pursue a specific direction which would ultimately bring me the most important quality of my life, *living in inner peace*.

Sometimes there's a belief that as a spiritual person we should allow some people, like parents, family, spouses, kids, etc., to betray us, and disrupt our inner peace, because, after all, we are the ones who are supposed to be loving, accepting, and spiritually mature. No way! I've come to realize that I am a direct part of this higher spiritual being that I dare call God, and I need to continue to honor that piece of me because of who I am and whose I am.

Understanding that, I will allow nobody to impose upon me any betrayal or any behavior that I deem to disrupt my inner peace. No matter who that person is. Not even my *m-o-t-h-e-r*.

Back in 2005, I thought that I was ready to begin to have a relationship with my mother. Very, very slowly I began to have contact with my mother and I truly thought I was in control of myself. My mother behaved for about four months because she realized that I was serious about taking care of myself. She acted very kind, staying out of my business, respecting my boundaries, and not being critical.

Slowly, but surely, she would go back to her criticism and judgment and gossip and complaining about people and situations. When I would tell her that it would not be tolerated, she would apologize and go back to a neutral subject. Within a couple of hours she would start to resume those same behaviors. I could manage only short visits with my mother in order to kid myself that if I didn't have a lot of contact with her, things would be ok.

Before too long, every time I spoke to her it would be exactly the same conversation. She would go back to very seething complaining, arguing, criticizing, judging, and gossiping. When I would tell her that I had become aware of other ways to handle those things that even she had acknowledged as negative, she stated very clearly that she did not want to make any changes and that she liked the way that she was. She would say that she was entitled to her opinion and I'd reply that I was entitled to not listen to them. She would give me the silent treatment for a few minutes and when she realized I was not going to engage, she would move on to another subject like nothing ever happened.

Fast forward to Easter weekend 2018. I scheduled a trip to visit my mom and three weeks before the trip my guts were churning, and my mind was racing about whether I really wanted to go through with the trip.

On the day of travel, my inner voice was screaming *You are done here*. You are done with her because you know nothing has changed, and nothing will change. It is ok to discontinue this relationship because it disturbs the core of you, which is your own inner peace. It's ok to protect your divinity.

As soon as I walked into her house I had an overwhelming knowing that I truly had completed with her and that there was no reason whatsoever to have any guilt or obligation over my decision. She truly had no hold on me anymore.

The most honoring thing I could have done for myself was to continue to support my divine place and myself. I spent two and a half unattached, neutral, and surreal days with her. By the end of the visit, she also acknowledged that we were done, although those words were not actually spoken during the visit.

I knew for certain that I would be walking away for the last time. I felt calm until I actually walked out and turned around and looked at her. She put on a pouty face and I turned away. I cried for a minute because of the old conditioning of guilt, but really more because I felt a loss. At the same time, I also felt relief that it was finally going to be over.

So now my older sister reports to me about how mom is doing. She is still riddled with guilt and feels responsible for visiting mom, even though she cannot stand talking to her, or even be in her presence.

FULL DISCLOSURE

I seriously doubt that it is lost on anybody that terminating a relationship, albeit toxic, with your mother or any other family member, will probably be very tough. Even if you are doing it for the right reasons, respecting your divinity and inner peace so that you can be of the best service to yourself and others, it is difficult. I realize that because we are human, it still has a lot of emotion behind it.

Earlier in this book I mentioned that having written this book, I immediately experienced the emotion of betrayal. Having worked so hard on betrayal issues between my mom and me, I was very surprised that it came up again. I also stated that I realized that the feeling of betrayal was the final feeling of betrayal that I was ever going to have in relation to her because I knew that I was finally terminating this relationship for the right reason.

One of the other things that I've found is that for me, it dipped again into grieving issues that I thought I had alleviated myself of over the years.

Our inner child hosts our self-esteem and can still have some latent issues even as we mature.

Even with my several decades of doing active processes, whether in seminar or self-help readings or sessions with other intuitive/spiritual healers, I found that the process of completing this relationship with my mother brought up a lot of grief that was still in me, and as it turned out, many things that I had been stuffing away.

This grief ended up being something that I was experiencing on a very subtle level, because either I was unwilling to recognize it, or it was so ingrained in me that I didn't realize that I was not taking care of myself. The grief was directly related to subconscious beliefs of my childhood years:

- My mom's love was conditional on me *behaving*
- I was not being nurtured or supported in my needs or development
- I was unacknowledged, disrespected, challenged, and redirected, all so my mom could be in control and in the limelight

And so, I masked my grief with sarcasm and anger.

I realized that we will give up our own fulfillment and happiness for the big picture, or for other people, because we feel that it is the right thing to do. What was coming up for me in the way of grief was how in my previous relationships I sacrificed everything to do with what I wanted and needed, and anything that was fully in support of myself and my happiness.

I was not raised a selfish person but I do believe that we have the right to be happy and to have our honorable desires fulfilled.

Know that it is honorable to take care of yourself. It is not selfish. It is you being of service to yourself so you can be of service to others.

It hasn't been that long since I finally started honoring what it is that I want and need and what will bring about my being the best and most honest me, what I was put on this planet to be.

As I began to write this book, I started to have symptoms that were similar to an intestinal virus. I do not believe in germ theory, especially since I had been keeping my immunity up, so I always look to see where the emotional or psychic level of the physical incident is from. It turned out to be all of the years that I had pushed down and swallowed the grief and the anger that I had, essentially from day one of my existence. And I had not yet uncovered and addressed it on the planet.

Here's the big takeaway: It is very probable that you too, if you choose to honor yourself and your divinity and your inner peace and choose to remove toxic people from your life, may have other emotions and inner processes come up for you.

It may seem odd, but I am actually grateful that the emotion of grief and the injured inner child came up for me again because I truly believe that everything we experience is something to learn and grow from.

The writing of this book, and anything else that I will be presenting, I am doing from a place of being part of my Ministry. I believe that as a minister I can help others by sharing my experiences from every level that I have embraced. I wish for you inner peace, acceptance, and freedom.

All things for the best and highest good of all concerned.

EPILOGUE: THIS DOCTOR RECOMMENDS

Doctor? While I am a Doctor in the healthcare field, I can also say that I am a Doctor of Life. With all the experiences that I have had and all the changes and growth along the way, I do feel uniquely qualified to claim that my life's experiences and training affords me the title of *Life Doctor*.

Here are some recommendations for completing uncomfortable, possibly unhealthy, relationships, no matter the title or status of the person:

* First, one of my favorite mottos: *Life is about interpretation and timing.* This is what I felt was my truth of experience.

* If we decide we need help, it is important to get professional help from sources that resonate with you. A therapist is often objective and can assist with identifying your realizations to inner conflict.

* Realize that making change and taking charge of your life so that you can have emotionally appropriate and healthy relationships can seem uncomfortable, if not initially emotionally painful.

* Create personal boundaries. Realize this probably won't be popular with those people who neither have nor recognize boundaries.

* Learn to be ok with saying *No*.

* Stay away from negativity, whether people or media.

* If need be, drop all of your current relationships that do not serve you and your wants/needs for the best and highest good.

* Consider other forms of personal/professional growth such as seminars, podcasts, videos, retreats, etc.

* Find tools to rid yourself of anything that comes up repeatedly because it may be limiting your life. For me, that was anger. Here's an example – I threw ice cubes at my brick house and watched them bust to pieces. My therapist wanted me to hit a tree with a baseball bat. I felt that would be an assault on the tree. And it would hurt me too!

* Lastly, get yourself as strong and clear and armed with true self-esteem as you can so that you terminate your toxic relationships from the standpoint of being truly comfortable with knowing and accepting that being done with those

relationships is what is absolutely necessary for your inner

peace, and that it is *not* done out of anger, fear, resentment,

hate, hope, or denial.

Made in the USA
Columbia, SC
20 January 2020